Understanding AI

Understanding AI

Leroy Vincent

Contents

1 Introduction   1
2 The Basics of Artificial Intelligence   3
3 Ethical Considerations in AI   7
4 AI in Various Industries   13
5 The Future of AI   19
6 Conclusion   23

Copyright © 2024 by Leroy Vincent
All rights reserved. No part of this book may be reproduced in any manner whatsoever without written permission except in the case of brief quotations embodied in critical articles and reviews.
First Printing, 2024

1
Introduction

Artificial intelligence (AI) has been widely talked about in recent years regarding the future of AI and the possible benefits and harms it could create. While many scientists and researchers have given ambiguous views, the discourse seems to evoke a set of questions and justifications. Why is understanding of AI even necessary? Where are we today concerning AI development and use? Which path to take? This essay seeks to persuade us to understand the significance of learning AI and to motivate it. We will elucidate some current research pathways and make some recommendations based on current status and research for AI trends whose development provides a brighter future.

To introduce this section, we explain the background of artificial intelligence. We learn how learning AI is relevant in the main section. The future discussion on AI will follow. The original formation of artificial intelligence addresses the digital replication of human thinking, ending up with the ramifying boughs of artificial cleverness and symbolic information processing. It is not surprising that the following important piece of the research is image-based problem solving. Vision is our richest sensory output, composed at core-cognition as classified of knowledge. Since the earliest moments of artificial intelligence, humans have been obsessed with the principle that our initial cognitive knowledge-how to connect subjective and objective data events also to accomplish tasks. Deep learning is an important step for reaching this functionality, though because it wants a wise technique, the end is still uncertain.

2

The Basics of Artificial Intelligence

Artificial Intelligence, or AI, needs no introduction. It is one of the most revolutionary technologies of the 21st century, and its capabilities are truly endless. However, before we delve deeper into AI, it's imperative that we understand the basics. AI is an intelligent machine or program which has the ability to solve computational and logical problems. It can perform the jobs of a human using cognitive processes like learning, understanding, reasoning, and implementing strategies. There are three types of AI - Narrow AI, General AI, and Super AI. Narrow AI is what we see all around us and is designed to perform a narrow task. They are intelligent machines that are not capable of performing other tasks beyond the one they are meant to do.

Machine Learning (ML) is a subset of AI, and Deep Learning (DL) is a type of ML. ML is a type of AI that is designed to learn and make predictions. It is very good at finding patterns in data that humans can't predict. Algorithms are the foundation of machine learning, and they are being used to train a machine to learn from a set of data. This is called a model. Once the model has been trained using a set of training data, it can then be used to make predictions. This is called inference. DL goes one step further. Rather than looking at the numbers in a spreadsheet, it looks at the raw data and looks for features that it can use to make decisions. It's like having a conversation with a human and asking them a series of questions. They may not know why they answered the way they did, but they know the answer because it is a general rule they have learned. DL works the same way, it learns from experience and doesn't require handcrafted features. It's able to process and understand data like images, sound, and text, and it's the thing that enables AI to communicate with humans.

Definition and Types of AI

Artificial intelligence is often referred to as "AI" and has been an interest to researchers and scholars for the last several decades. To put it in simple terms, AI refers to the concept of machines that are capable of carrying out tasks that generally require some form of intelligence in humans. In machines, these tasks are often carried out through complex sets of instructions, algorithms, and data processing.

The future of AI will show symptoms of this concept in the development of machines that are capable of taking in human commands and reformulating them in an optimal manner, embodying logical and inductive reasoning to some extent, understanding and evaluating complex issues, and learning from their environment and experiences. This type of system is called strong AI, where machines with consciousness and emotions resonate with human intelligence, and has not yet been fully developed.

One of the most important factors in the processing ability of AI systems is their knowledge base, which refers to the database an AI system has accumulated through its experiences or otherwise. There is more than one way to classify AI systems. According to the decision-making and problem-solving capabilities of these systems, AI systems are divided into two general categories: weak or specialized AI and strong or general AI. Weak AI systems (or narrow AI) are designed to carry out a relatively simple sequence of tasks based on human commands. The complexity of a task a weak AI system carries out can vary from behavior-based robotic systems to facial recognition software used in personal computers.

Another categorization of AI systems is dependent upon their capabilities and application areas. For instance, AI systems based on their characteristics can be either intelligent agents or nonintelligent AI systems.

Machine Learning and Deep Learning

Despite the range of definitions of AI presented earlier, it is apparent that in broader terms, AI encompasses the comprehensive tooling of empowered computers. However, the computer and its ancillary software alone are not AI; it entirely relates to how these systems are fitted and programmed such that they can successfully mimic or engender humanly perceptible responses. One method is machine learning: the process of training AI systems or deep learning models with a vast amount of data. These algorithms enable machines to learn from data, identify situations, and make decisions without, or with minimal, human intervention.

The AI of today is based on data-driven learning and decision-making, which uses machine learning or advanced deep learning statistics. Such a model becomes more intelligent as it is given more data to train on. This all begins with an analytical model: a representation of information in a form that can be used for decision-making. Through historical data, an AI engine will examine such models and use them to distinguish account trends, characteristics, or footprints of complex incidents such as unexpected economic shifts or patterns of fraudulent behavior. Once the model maker is formed, it is fully ready as an AI manager. Oftentimes, however, unlike most of the statistical software intelligence-based manager randomly comes active by random events, machine learning systems do not need hand-coded decisions since they frame decisions alone using historical data.

3

Ethical Considerations in AI

As AI moves from concept to reality, increasingly exciting potential applications are emerging. However, our understanding of it is far from complete. In response to the widespread deployment of AI, issues and ethical considerations have been raised, suggesting that this new technology could pose unique risks to society.

Issues and ethical considerations have been raised as AI becomes widespread in industry and society. The ability of AI systems to solve complex tasks might instigate a shift in the global workforce, leading to concerns about different types of biases and fairness. These concerns originate from the learning process of AI systems and how these systems are first trained on historical data before being deployed. This historical data reflects human prejudices and societal inequalities. Privacy and security are also important for successful AI developments. There is widespread concern around increased surveillance and erosion of privacy. Data management and privacy are of particular importance during the implementation of personal assistants and conversational AI technology. Increasingly sophisticated conversational AI systems have the potential to exchange highly personal and sensitive information with end-users. There is an ethical responsibility to properly monitor and evaluate who is collecting and handling this data.

Facial recognition has rapidly become an unacceptable application in AI and many organizations are banning the use of the technology. AI is also capable of generating fake personal information and voices, known as deepfakes. The creation and distribution of deepfakes have important implications for privacy and trust. As deepfakes continue to develop, society's need for evaluating what is trustworthy information also increases. This is more than ever an ethical consideration. Furthermore, as progress accelerates, the principles that govern the use of proprietary AI algorithms are still yet to be fully established. This has considerable implications for end-users. Full awareness of AI capabilities should be made clear within accompanying user agreements. It is currently unclear what precautions should be taken regarding the spread of harmful AI. The misuse of AI could help humans commit crime, manage disasters, or undertake novel military tactics. Collectively, there are few platforms and methodologies in place for academic, industry, and government-level discussion on responsible AI. As AI systems develop and improve, the need for these options escalates.

Bias and Fairness

Despite their increasing capacity and use, AI systems are built using models and algorithms that are not free from human fallibility. The data fed into these systems, often created or collected by people, contain systemic biases, which can manifest themselves in the results of AI systems. It is therefore important to be aware of these issues and to address them in the development of AI systems. Such considerations also introduce biases or prejudices into AI systems as well. AI technology highlights the impact of these traits, and as such these topics are active research areas.

Fairness in AI has been explored on multiple levels. One example is the fairness/injustice of the predictions of AI (e.g., not hiring a person for no other reason than that many people of their gender/ethnic background/etc have not performed well in that role). Another is the use of AI for decision-making in criminal justice, where the stakes are very high (decisions about risk assessments or predicting recidivism). We cannot address these issues in full here, but we will mention some examples of unfairly biased AI that we should pay attention to. In 2016, a controversy broke out revealing that the datasets of Amazon, Canon, HP, and IBM contained symbols that were forgotten more often if paired with female names. The AI reflected the qualities of the people collecting the data. Prior to this, in 2014, Amazon built a recruitment algorithm which penalized any CV that contained the word "woman" or descriptions of women's sports or was from being part of a women's association.

In China, the services giant Shenzhen was found in July 2018 to be using a score, built with data from major Russian company Ntechlab, to judge the potential to commit a terrorist crime by one or more people with a 7 per cent (a "certain probability"). While the score depended in part on whether "hiding from the public or neighbors" and "reluctant to 'communicate with others, rejection of vague and ambiguous conversations" were characteristic of someone, other features were deeply coded with bias. The profile of a terrorist that represented a major sequence in the algorithm was 18 to 23 "disgruntled" individuals who do not look people in the eye, who buy matchsticks or remote-controlled toys instead of smart washing machines ("nervousness"), switch internet cafes to do their banking (a potential wealthy, law-abiding person would bank regularly, from the office or their home), not take calls from Bank call center to confirm their identity, and apply earlier in the day and without caveat for a cash loan to buy plane tickets to a US city up to 6000km from Beijing ("without a valid reason for travel"). Furthermore, the confidence that Shenzhen had in this highly controversial AI was illustrated in the fact that in Shenzhen's "increasing scores" the interview was conducted without paying any attention to the evidence or security risk posed by these individuals. Aside from concerns about the false positives and disruption of impressionable, nervous young people growing up in China, there are concerns over bias in weighting certain behavioral indicators in their AI model. This use of the technology in this way represents both a very polarizing possible outcome, and a clear violation of independently-determined ethical best practice.

Privacy and Data Security

Privacy and Data Security. At their core, AI applications are about processing accumulated knowledge and orchestrating the mass data available to identify the suitable paths to follow. It is a form of synthetic science informed by the data subject's physical, psychic, and social circumstances. The daunting numerical volume and principal shapeless state of the typical data pool virtually demand that there is no human expert who can access it personally. That is why, when dealing with AI, privacy is a significant issue. Quite frequently, there is no obvious or comprehensible logic between the initial data and the final result due to the multiple strata of an AI solution, which render it nearly inexplicable.

Regardless, we see the related theoretical standing between privacy and security. They are both essential aspects of the basic human right to freedom of creative action. Privacy, anyway, appears to be the more delicate concept, as it is more likely to be "side by side" or antagonistic to the related freedom security objective, as Johann Remmel argues. According to Nigel Dimmock, humans exchange some security for privacy while purchasing products or engaging in online activity. Of course, if the privacy/security duality is adopted in individual circumstances, the biases are not the same – public space surveillance or based on biographic factors which can accidentally detect some security threats, as a result acting against the legitimate interests of the person scrutinized, which includes the loss of privacy within the activities of security agencies. Without respect for the protection of privacy, the balance between measures for protecting security that are proportionate and measures that are excessive and inappropriately infringe on human rights will be thrown off.

4
AI in Various Industries

AI is already playing a critical role in healthcare, helping doctors assess patients and detect a wide variety of diseases. AI systems are being developed that analyze scans from MRI, CT, and PET machines, which can be quicker and cheaper than an in-person analysis from a doctor. In addition to scans, AI is also helping doctors better understand their patients at the molecular level by analyzing data from genomics and proteomics. Despite the magic-like abilities AI systems have shown when interpreting data, they do not make diagnoses on their own even today. AI systems give doctors suggestions when asked, but in the end, it is entirely up to the doctor to make the final call and make the diagnosis. AI can now correlate a patient's history with how they responded to different treatment in the past and predict how they will respond to different treatments in the future.

Many major retail banks are already employing AI systems to detect fraud in payment transactions. AI's ability to synthesize large amounts of data quickly makes it particularly well-suited for fraud detection, and it is often incorporated into digital marketplaces and data centers. Meanwhile, more recent improvements in neural networks have also made AI a very powerful tool for distinguishing spam from non-spam. AI systems can often accurately identify whether an email containing links or attachments that are common in phishing campaigns. In the future, it may also be used to search the web to associate, classify, aggregate, and manage IoT data.

Healthcare

In healthcare, AI is expanding new frontiers for revolutionizing healthcare delivery, diagnostics, personalized medicines, and public health. With AI, it is now possible to track and predict disease occurrence and outbreaks, personalize medicines, develop new therapies, and even differentiate normal and abnormal behaviors from human-patient-generated data. Physicians, with the help of AI, can now make decisions more accurately and efficiently. Modern AI techniques such as machine learning, deep learning, and reinforcement learning allow AI to capture behavioral patterns of diseases that may not be easy to detect using traditional statistics or other methods.

AI offers increasing opportunities for everything from machine learning to predictive analytics in health services research and is becoming a fundamental part of consumer health companies, making care and services more convenient, increasing personal health through wearables and self-monitoring, and improving adherence and access for behavioral health treatment. AI technologies, such as machine learning, natural language processing, and robotics, present an array of potential new tools for healthcare benefits, companies that offer an opportunity to significantly improve new generations and populations. Meanwhile, AI presents opportunities to enhance areas in healthcare decisions, including diagnosis and diagnostic imaging technologies. However, despite its transformative power in healthcare, concerns have been raised that AI has the potential to disrupt healthcare delivery models and be only available to wealthier health systems and providers. Ethical questions have also been raised about the uses of AI, including patient privacy, consent, and the uses of data, as well as concerns about institutional accountability for its use.

Finance

In finance, AI has the capability for transforming the consumer finance experience, helping us to make better and more empowered decisions as consumers in the future. It can help us to predict and manage our own personal finances, optimizing our spending, saving, investment, and borrowing for our specific goals and lifestyles, even under extreme stresses. Banks and financial services can leverage AI for risk management, such as automating the assessment of small business loan applications, gaining real-time insights into counter-party credit risk, and personalizing financial advice. AI can also be used for faster fraud detection, automatically adjust customers' lending rates and limits according to credit history, purchase patterns, and social network data, and optimize invoice processing and trade finance operations. However, there is a combination of considerable ethical, legal, and operational problems to solve, which if solved effectively could unleash a step change in value added.

The development of AI and other data-driven technologies has had an extraordinary impact on the finance industry across a range of functions, including commercial banking, markets, and investment, insurance and pensions. Global institution members of the World Economic Forum (WEF) valued their deployment of AI at USD 122 billion in 2018 and are projecting this to increase to USD 4.87 trillion in 2022 – before taking full account of the impact of the pandemic. In the data-driven disruption of FinTech more generally, revenues of digitally-disruptive Challenger Banks in the UK were growing by an average of 80–200% p.a. up to 2019. A study in 2019 found that US consumers were more likely to share their financial data or use services from technology companies in AI, cloud, big data, and blockchain, which have more scope to invert knowledge-based markets for customer finance, e.g. insurance for connected cars. Recognizing this looming disruption and heralding a post execution paradigm a Chief Digital Officer of Prudential Distribution which manages a USD 90 billion business globally was quoted in the global press as saying "we are no longer an insurance company. We are a revolving data company".

Transportation

Various transportation innovations are being devised with the help of AI. A few of them are autonomous vehicles (AVs), Traffic Management Systems (TMS), "Mobility as a Service" (MaaS), Decentralized logistic systems (LIP) for efficient and secure transportation, etc. The introduction of AVs will provide mobility for people with limited mobility, increase the safety of transportation, and reduce ecological problems like pollution. Traffic Management Systems (TMS) are systems that provide useful actions for avoiding congestion, road accidents, accidents occurring while working with heavy machines like cranes in construction sites, or any other vehicle-related incidents on the road. "Mobility as a Service" (MaaS) can be defined as a platform or an on-demand service that integrates end-to-end trip services across all modes of transportation in a single digital PaaS (Platform as a Service) ecosystem, allowing users to create a tailor-made trip using different types of transportation services (public and semi-public).

Decentralized logistics systems (LIPs) are logistics transportation systems that use Blockchain technology to get their transportation services and coordinate their transportation activities. The major components in this system are: AVs, TMS, 5G networks, GPS (Global Positioning Systems), IoT (Internet of Things), Blockchain, Cryptocurrency, Smart Contracts, Logistic service marketplace for logs. Societies can get immediate transportation services in a cost-efficient way because the LIP-based system is a manual system in which everyone needs to get some consignments or deliver some consignment for some amount. This information is printed on paper and distributed to the employees so that everyone knows to whom they want to send the consignments and from whom they want to take the consignments. The ethical impact of the AI-based system in transportation is: how much accuracy does the AI system infuse into decision-making while working with the crowd? While considering security and handling accidents, how does AI make decisions, and what is the long-term and short-term impact of the decisions made by AI? Ethical utilization of resources and handling accidents.

Autonomous Vehicles: AVs use a computer-based system to control all their operations like driving, starting, and stopping. They use a communication system to inform all other co-related cars and traffic signals about their actions. The main advantage of AVs is that they reduce travel time, increase safety, reduce fuel consumption, and address traffic issues. Autonomous Cargo Delivery: They are mainly used for transporting goods from city centers to final destinations and can carry about 450 kg of load. These delivery vans travel 15 miles (24.1 km) during the day and 7 miles (11.2 km) at night. Smart Traffic Lights and Intelligent Transportation Systems (ITS): Various smart traffic lights are interconnected and coordinated to avoid traffic jams. Intelligent Vehicles (AVs) determine if they can stop or slow down when they detect red-light signals and adjust their speed according to different green lights ahead. They also predict weather and traffic patterns to adjust speed. Public Transit Systems, Smart Cities, and Transportation Data: Smart cities use smart wireless drives, smart steering wheels, and smartware connected to phones. Smart Charge Infrastructure: The AI algorithm uses data to predict the charging habits of individuals and enables it to predict when electric-driven vehicles will be available for charging. Ethical considerations include justice, deployment, social, and economic factors.

5

The Future of AI

AI development is rapidly changing these days, and what is typically referred to as the future of AI today will soon become the norm. As automation is rapidly getting smarter, we can expect it to reflect on the current and future workplace as well.

It is widely expected that AI will lead technological innovation by a vast margin in the next decade. Today, the advancements in AI research and engineering are catalyzing new capabilities across high-value industry sectors. The future of industrial automation systems will be dependent on AI systems working seamlessly with a similar level of cognitive functions like human beings. Various workshops and seminars on AI and robotics are held annually. Most of these mediums of exchange highlight global AI machinery and automation systems as future platforms for the data-driven and smart industries envisaged. Over the three decades, these seminars show twenty-four percent of generated AI patents. While the number is relatively low, it is evident that more inventors are coming up with disruptive AI technologies and avenues for commercialization. In the long term, these disruptions could open up independent pathways for the technology. In addition, some of these systems are already here - across a wide variety of industry applications. The bulk of R&D components are situated in their modules to enhance productivity and operational synergism. As of today, global artificial intelligence machinery productivity is still heavily used within the following application areas, inter alia: service robots which are rapidly becoming popular and are revolutionizing the service industry globally.

The concept of industrial automation can be regarded as a combination of automation technologies and digital control strategies that perform industrial processes without human intervention. The field has experienced an exponential leap in digital real-time control and data processing capabilities to such an extent that it began to be known as Cyber-Physical Systems. Modern technology has demonstrated an increased ability to interconnect separate embedded systems to communicate and cooperate within themselves and with the environment surrounding it. Cyber-Physical System developments are usually used in numerous industrial sectors such as raw materials processing, manufacturing of the final products, design and development, storage and retrieval in warehouses, and national distribution systems. Automating industrial processes can result in cost reductions, material savings, improved quality, increased profitability, higher consistency and manufacturing traceability, enhanced process flexibility and efficiency, and lower energy consumption. Case in point, the global artificial intelligence machinery market was valued at 3.3 billion dollars in 2016 and is expected to exhibit a cumulative annual growth rate (CAGR) of 43.8 percent in the forecast period 2017-2026.

Advancements in AI Research

Advancements in AI Research. Recent advancements in AI research have generated a plethora of enhanced capabilities in areas like natural language processing, conversational AI, vision and perception, generative model design, among others, which already have been, and in the foreseeable future will continue to, meaningfully impact our field. This massive explosion of introduction of so many significant advances may actually partly explain why we may have seen halts in the AI winter reports, but also give us an idea of the possible future landscape of AI, if many of the developments that have happened since the latest survey of AI trends will lead to relevant and widely used applications. Currently, some of the overall topic developments in 2020-2021 include advancements in making pretrained language models more efficient, through techniques like distillation and heavier parameter pruning; a sharper focus on multimodal machine learning; a lot of creative work in adversarial ("robust") AI; "vision" Transformers; fundamental new directions in generative deep learning, in part introduced through the exceptional successes of GPT-3; good results in AI-assisted drug discovery and protein structure.

The other avenue through which to catch a glance at placing our expectations is forward-looking surveys or trend spotlights, in the form of long and short "lens" pieces, that were at the time of publishing quite current in showing us glimpses of the future. In a recent, open book-like survey, released by Google DeepMind, a number of experts and pioneers in AI are interviewed and asked to give their opinions on the most interesting directions and current trends in AI research, which gives an interesting, prospective insight. Similarly, Salesforce's in November 2021 released survey compiles a lot of current survey data to project forwards a series of major AI and ML trends in the years to come.

AI and Automation

The integration of AI technologies with automation stands out as one of the defining features of the ongoing technological change potentially shaping future society. Emphasizing the close link between AI and automation, this publication puts the emphasis on the potential impact of future developments in these areas in numerous sectors and domains of life. As powerful drivers of change, automation and AI will be instrumental in reshaping homes and cities, industry and service sectors. New sectors are likely to emerge and older economies will get reshaped. The composition and conditions of work and workplaces are likely to get altered and formal and informal learning will span a longer period of the population's life. The AI-defined shift in automation will have significant, but not necessarily standard economic impact.

The integration of AI and automation - ACID for short - will see the alteration of economies and societies. Automation and AI will become the new normal, as software and machines carry out ever more analysis, drawing on ever larger new data sets, providing support for humans to carry out better decisions and actions. Through automation, AI will have an increasing impact on the workforce and work-related activities and thus on the occupational skills. Automation through AI will also be linked to a revision of institutional arrangements - from the design of industrial processes to that of the welfare state. As such, ACID is both an economic opportunity and something that raises a wide range of ethical issues.

6

Conclusion

With each new technological advancement, we open the doors to create things that were previously unimaginable. Drones, robots, cellphones, transportation systems, and medical equipment are all being developed with the help of AI. Business, education, industry, government, science, entertainment, and the military have all embraced the unique tools and gadgets associated with AI. It is now important to understand how one can guide the further development and application of artificial intelligence effectively and humanely.

One reason to study the future of AI is that we are currently in the midst of a new wave of AI. Arguably, AI research has changed radically over the last few years. Ideas from the early days of AI that were abandoned in the 1980s and 1990s have been revived, reformulated, and the methods enhanced with the increase in computational resources. OpenAI senior researcher Dario Amodei anticipates that we will see "systems that exhibit more sophisticated forms of generalization than current systems are capable of," "progress on systems that can learn from smaller datasets," and "progress on systems that can exhibit a broader range of prosocial behavior" in the near future. Some computer scientists believe the capabilities of these systems will develop explosively, with relatively sudden 'breakthroughs' leading to decisions which may have catastrophic consequences. Within the AI community, there is significant support for the idea that we are on the brink, or already in the midst, of an AI revolution. Policymakers are taking notice of the potential for harm—and the need to govern the technology intentionally.

www.ingramcontent.com/pod-product-compliance
Lightning Source LLC
LaVergne TN
LVHW092102060526
838201LV00047B/1536